ELIZABETH HANLY DANFORTH

FIREWOOD

And

Other Verse

By

Elizabeth Hanly Danforth

Illustrated by
CHARLES D. HUBBARD

Foreword by
WILBERT SNOW

FALMOUTH PUBLISHING HOUSE

Portland, Maine

ACKNOWLEDGMENT

Thanks are hereby extended to: *Bangor Daily News, Boston Transcript, The Outlook, The New York Times, Contemporary Verse, The Youth's Companion, The New York Sun, The Bookman, Spirit, The Survey, Blue Book—Maine, Book News Monthly, The Ladies' World, The New Yorker, Good Housekeeping* and *The Christian Science Monitor,* in which a great many of these poems first appeared.

"In A World Grown Timid I Think Of You."

FOREWORD

In 1939 Elizabeth Hanly Danforth's first book of poems, *In Rio on the Ouvidor,* was well received by the critics and has now run through three printings. The book was introduced by Kathleen Norris who wrote: "I defy anyone to read some of these verses without that sudden chill of sheer delight. . ." Mrs. Danforth loved the heart-warming life of Brazil where her husband was engaged in business. The color of South American landscapes and the Brazilian people charmed her imagination, and in the book she interpreted the region of Rio to her friends and readers in the North.

At her death Mrs. Danforth left the material for another book. This time the much-travelled poet strikes a nostalgic note—a love for the Maine seaport of her early formative years. The book opens with a tribute to Maine country life as exemplified by the activities on the wood lot in winter. She remembers with marvellous accuracy the details of wood chopping and the men who wielded the axe. The fragrances of the winter wood are in the poem "Firewood" and the memory of her father as a woodcutter expands into a tribute to all Maine men who figured so impressively in her childhood. She remembers the Civil War veterans at their Memorial Day exercises and links the war between the States with World War I that touched her own life poignantly and made an indelible impression on her. She lays laurel wreaths on her college friends who yielded their lives in Flanders. One of this group is a tribute to Raoul Lufberry, the American ace, whom she admired affectionately. She remembers her mother's flower garden and writes about it with minute attention to individual plants and flowers. In one of these she imagines her mother coming back from Paradise to look after her neglected garden. These flower and garden poems themselves are a notable part of the book.

She sings the charms of the little town of Thomaston—one of the loveliest towns in Maine. She remembers:

The land breeze freshening at close of day,
The chuckle of dark water round the piers,
Fog on our faces with the taste of tears,
The lighthouse flashing, fading down the bay.

At times she is so in love with Thomaston as she looks back on it from her home in Rio that she cries out:

Oh given choice of Heaven
I think my tired feet
Foregoing pearls and jasper
Would find this village street.

In another lyric, "Song for a Little Town," she gives this idealization a new Emily Dickinson twist:

I'll go again up Main Street
And there I'll lay me down.
Heaven a far, fair city?
Heaven's a little town.

There is love of the adventure of travel in these poems and she sings the praises of the Caribbean Islands as well as those of South America. Robert Louis Stevenson, the prince of adventurers, was one of her favorite authors. She writes with insight and gusto about the Irish characters of her home town and "Requiescat" and "Barney Glynn" are two poems that one will not soon forget.

She is essentially a lyricist and the Celtic ingredients of her nature give her poems their distinctive color. The Irish sadness that haunts the *Londonderry Air* is in her verse. At the close of "Question" she boldly cries out:

> *If Love can die, how will God keep*
> *The promise that all music makes?*

There is a freshness in the figures of her love lyrics that is not, perhaps, present in her other poems—fine as they are. For example, in the sonnet "I have no Wish to Claim Your Love" she writes:

> *I saw a woman once who gave her child*
> *To those who swore to love it as their own.*
> *Her voice was gentle and her gesture mild.*
> *She kissed its cheek and went away alone*
> *But I could guess, although she gave no sign,*
> *The voice that clamored in her heart, "Mine!*
> *Mine!"*

Technically Mrs. Danforth is traditional. Her affinities are with the English and American poets of the nineteenth century and the poets of the American poetic revival of 1912-1920. The non-emotional and anti-emotional poetry of the ultra moderns meant absolutely nothing to her. The beauty of the world moved her deeply. The last lines of her sonnet "Windy Morning"— (included in her first volume, entitled "In Rio on the Ouvidor") —about a young god who might:

> Stand for a moment, spellbound, half-afraid
> Before the beauty of a world he made

describe her attitude. If ever anyone was in love with this green earth it was the girl we knew as Beth Hanly. She sings the glories of an earth she loves and celebrates its people. Her range extends from a poem on the "Beauty of Youth" to one entitled "In Praise of Old Ladies," and in this latter poem she reveals herself in the couplet:

> But most of all I love old eyes
> Not too intent on Paradise.

This warm love of hers fills her friends with a desire to have her poetry better known to North Americans. Her work has been published in the *Cornhill Magazine,* the *Outlook,* the *Ladies' Home Journal* and in several anthologies, such as *The Best Poems of* 1935 selected by Thomas Moult (Jonathan Cape, London & Toronto), Anthology of *Magazine Verse* for 1916 and 1918 by William Stanley Braithwaite (Lawrence J. Gomme, New York) etc. But in the North she has never enjoyed the vogue she deserves. Mrs. Danforth's fine poetry should become better known and more widely appreciated, and such delightful poems as "Windy Morning" in the first book and "Nocturne" in this book should find their way into the anthologies. Meanwhile all of

Mrs. Danforth's friends owe a debt of gratitude to her husband, Mr. Stephen P. Danforth, for the care he has taken with her manuscripts and for the opportunity he has given us to enjoy *Firewood and Other Verse.*

Let me close with a quatrain entitled "Signature" which expresses in brief her fine qualities as a poet:

While little men revile His name,
And cynics scoff and fools deny,
God seals the year in maple flame,
And scrawls the wild geese on the sky.

WILBERT SNOW,
Wesleyan University
Middletown, Connecticut

CONTENTS
Part One

FIREWOOD 3
SUMMER'S END 9
AUTUMN HOME-COMING 11
WHEN I HEAR TALK OF GARDENS . . 12
THIRD GENERATION 14
HER GARDEN 16
LAVENDER 19
OUR GARDEN 20
NEW ENGLAND PORT 21
HOME 24
HEPATICAS 25
LITTLE ROADS 26
SONG FOR A LITTLE TOWN 28
RETURN TO THE FARM 30
MAIN STREET 32
SIGNATURE 33
ARRIVAL 34
PUSSY-WILLOWS 36
THE SECRET 38
HOME TREASURE 40
WET STREETS 41
ALIEN 42
SECRET 44
DICKSONIA AND SWEET-FERN . . . 45
REQUIESCAT 46
BARNEY GLYNN 48

Part Two

MEMORIAL DAY 51
FOR RAOUL LUFBERRY 52

News Reel 53
Pursuit 54
The Wireless Station 55
Paradox 56
Alan Seeger 58
Fulfillment 59
Hymn 60
November Eleventh 61
Death of A Sportsman 62
April, 1917 63
First To Fall 64
Trees Of Picardy 65
Back Home 66
For A Cantonment Library . . . 67
In An Old Graveyard 68
The Paradox 70
A Prayer 71
"Unfit For Service" 72
Yale Campus 73
Amende 74
Out of The Dark 76
Broadcast 78
"And It Is Not Well To Tarry At The
Gods' Feast" 80
Nostalgia 81

Part Three

Lad 84
Profession 85
Discovery 87
De Profundis 88
Arraignment 89

CARPE NOCTEM	90
AFTER STORM	91
CONFESSION	92
GREETING	93
THE WOODS ROAD	94
FULFILLMENT	95
PERVERSE	96
HOME-COMING	97
THE BETTER PART	98
THE SNAPSHOT	100
"I HAVE NO WISH TO CLAIM YOUR LOVE . . ."	101
APRIL TIDE	102
REMINDER	103
THE "IMITATIONS"	104
EYES THAT HAVE HELD MY HEAVEN . . .	105
CHALLENGE	106
QUESTION	107
A HAWAIIAN RECORD	108
HER RING	109
THIRST	110
HOUSE O'DREAMS	113
THE PROVENCAL SPEAKS	114
INTERVAL	115
NIGHT CLUB	116
SONG	117
TO COPHETUA'S BEGGAR MAID	118
TO A REALIST	120
SIXTEEN	122
TO R.L.S.	124
IN PRAISE OF OLD LADIES	127
REAGENT	128

MY BOYS 129

AN ODE FOR THE DIAMOND JUBILEE OF

    MOUNT DE CHANTAL 130

MY WISH 132

ASPIRATIONS 133

FRIENDS 134

NOCTURNE 135

MY GRAVE 136

COMPANIONSHIP 137

BEAUTY OF YOUTH 138

FIREFLIES 140

NEXT DOOR 141

CLOSING 142

INTO THE NIGHT 143

AT 123RD STREET, EAST 144

CONVALESCENT 146

CATHEDRAL DOORWAY 147

SPORT O'KINGS 148

MOVIE MAGIC 150

A CHRISTMAS CARD 151

NEW LAMPS 152

FIREWOOD

And

OTHER VERSE

Part One

FIREWOOD
(To G. V. H.)

"Six weeks' sledding in March . . . "
And the sound of an axe in the frosty air.
"So-and-so's cutting," his neighbors say,
Felling the hardwood here and there
Thriftily, as New England knows.

Day after solitary day,
Swinging his luncheon bucket he goes,
Purposeful, sturdy, and alone,
Trudging along the pasture road
Ghostly with last year's faded bloom.
Ice has prisoned the boughs that arch
Bending under their feathery load
And fashioned a secret, shadowy room
Where rabbit tracks have patterned the snows
And the squirrel scattered a dry pine cone.

Siskins move in a lisping flock
From bough to bough of the yellow larch.
Kinglets flutter, and somber crows
Caw, while the bluejay curious
Screams from the balsam's topmost spire.

Woodsman, true to country code,
He spares the rare and rusty spray
That will bear the miracle, arbutus,
When he clears the moss and twigs away
From a level space on the sunny rock,

And snaps in two the crackling briar,
Lopping the branches, piling them up
Into a heap for his noonday fire.

"Hew," his adage, "to the line."
So his axe is sunk that the tree may fall
With a sliding, accurate, muffled, crash,
Down the hillside, toward the light.
Nothing here of tasseled pine,
Hacmatac or juniper,
Poverty-bitten spruce, or fir
Blazed for cutting at Christmas time;
But maple and oak tree past their prime,
Sweet wild cherry and stubborn ash,
Smooth clean beech with its thin gold leaves
Holding the summer in them still,
Silver birch, and yellow, and white
With its curling bark for the extra cup
That berry-pickers fill.

Sleigh bells jangling clear and bold,
The "sweet weather" call of the chickadee.
Grating of runners past the ledge,
Snicker of squirrels from tree to tree,
Peering down from a vantage nook
At the steaming horse in the trampled snow,
And the mittened figures clumsy with cold
Piling the logs on the wooden sledge.

Pussy-willows by every brook,
Snow in the hollows, wild geese high.

And freed, when the logs are pulled apart,
A Mourning-cloak, a butterfly
First of the year's bright brotherhood,
Breaks from its dusky prison hid
Wintry months in the old oak's heart,
Hovers and folds its wings and sips
Where a stain of sap shows wet and dark,
Spring-sweet, upon the maple bark.
The grainy sawdust whirls and drips
From the saw's keen teeth, and the fragrant
    chips
Leap from the axe-blade's swift attack.
Robins are calling, ploughing begun.
And twilight by twilight, a thrifty stack
Of clean, symmetrical, quartered wood
Climbs to a heartening pyramid
To be seasoned daily by wind and sun.

The second crop of clover is mown,
Grass grown tall in the old woods road,
Goldenrod faded in every rut.
Haying is over and harvest done,
Barns are filled and the swallows flown,
Gentians blue in the marshes still.
Brush for the banking must be cut,
And apples go to the cider mill.

Haying is over and harvest done
In Hope and Union and Appleton,
Little and lovely and honest places,
(I name you over, one by one)
St. George, Liberty, Thomaston.

In a world grown timid I think of you,
Your small white houses, your mighty barns,
Your berry pastures that once I knew,
Your stony fields with their browsing sheep,
Your strong old men with their quiet faces,
And the green graveyards where my people
    sleep.

Kingdoms waver. Empires fall.
Summers blossom and summers pass.
Apples gleam in the orchard grass
And the year grows tragic and tired and old.
But the men that I know the best of all,
Old Maine men with patient faces,
Their wood stands heaped like a fortress wall,
Their children sleep in quiet chambers,
Their fires burn against the cold.
Their rooms are sweet with the smell of birch
Rough to the touch with its curling bark.
Their sheds are stacked with maple and oak,
Their windows are ruddy in the dark.
Blow by blow and stroke by stroke,
Gnarled and deft and tireless hands
Have raised these roof-trees, walled these lands,
Have shaped a destiny to their will
Till it stands four-square to every shock.
There is flame at the heart of the granite rock,
They are strong with a strength beyond our
    ken.
God be praised for New England men!

SUMMER'S END

"Swallows gather on the wires,
Traveler's joy has gone to seed.
Twists of smoke go up from little fires
Through the orchard, down the pasture lane.
A little while your meadow larks again
Can flash across blue water and brown reed.
In their perfection would that you might heed
The first red leaf, the last blue gentian flower,
Asters regal in the brief, bright hour
Traveler's joy has gone to seed."

This your message that I read.
Some day when my gypsy gods turn kind,
All my vagabonding left behind,
I'll seek that quiet lane of old desires,
Follow where the homing star shall lead.
But when swallows gather on the wires,
Blessed, lay your hand across my eyes,
Lest you read there how my heart denies, denies,
Traveler's joy can go to seed.

AUTUMN HOME-COMING

Brown harvest fields and grey stone-walls,
Rose-hips and yellowing fern-frond;
Still pools that catch the sunset gold,
Velvet squares of furrowed mould,
Blue, gentle hills beyond.

Green waves that crash in opal foam,
Pine forests faithful to the sea;
Old pastures silvery with yew,
Forgotten pathways winding through
Green clumps of bayberry.

Oh, since God made us out of earth,
Glad, glad am I to come from these:
Ashes of triumphant pyres,
Maple, oak, and sumach fires,
Autumn's clean ecstasies!

Dust of the road my sons will go,
Dust of the ways my fathers trod.
Limestone and granite chipped by sea,
Stanch in the very bone of me,
Stand to Thy praise, O God!

WHEN I HEAR TALK OF GARDENS

When I hear talk of gardens,
I think of one I know
Where pink, beruffled hollyhocks
Go quaintly in a row
Past lovely Lady Larkspur,
Whose beauty takes the breath,
And poppies in their dancing
Disdain to-morrow's death.

About its walls the snowdrops
Crowd earliest in spring.
It boasts a gray old lattice
Where yellow roses cling;
Three stone steps, a cedar,
A woodbine arch where through
You glimpse our glad green meadowlands
And far hills softly blue.

When I hear talk of gardens,
It seems I breathe again
The hopeful, wholesome fragrance
Of new mould dark with rain.
My heart leaps up in laughter
When lilac buds are tossed,
Or ruddy gold chrysanthemums
Grow bittersweet with frost.

I know how purple foxgloves
Crowd past its iron gate;
Why junco-birds come early
And whitethroats linger late.
Sometimes gulls go over
Drifting toward the sea
Where come soft winds and silver mists
To walk caressingly.

When I hear talk of gardens,
Great gardens oversea,
That poets love to sing of,
I wonder can they be
More gracious to the spirit
Than this one that I know,
Where pink, beruffled hollyhocks
Go quaintly in a row.

THIRD GENERATION

The prim front door stands open wide,
Bright sunlight lies along the floor,
Blue smoke curls upward from the hearth,
For life is in the house once more.

Youth, hope, and laughter praise the place,
The handiwork of love, their host,
But sometimes in the summer dark
A thrifty little Irish ghost

I think must walk these rooms she knew,
To note with calm approving eyes
Cupboard shelves and braided rugs,
And patchwork quilts and draperies.

And on the door-sill in the dawn,
She will pause before she goes,
To clap her soft old palms and rout
With Gaelic threats, the Yankee crows.

HER GARDEN

We had no heart, remembering her,
To seek her lonely garden place
Fearing at every step to miss
The eager little face;

The garden hat soon thrown aside,
The broad low brow without a fleck,
The vagrant little curls that clung
About a sunburned neck;

The gingham apron stained with mould
About the stooping, slender form,
The hand that plied the weeding fork
With care for workman worm.

Incredible it seemed when she
Forgot her flowers and went away,
The garden still could flaunt and flame
Indifferent and gay.

Nasturtium glory waxed and waned,
The woodbine, with none there to see,
Enwrapped a saucy scarlet arm
About the cedar tree.

Last night we sat before the hearth
While winds were cold and rains were rude,
We sought the garden paths at dawn
In swift solicitude.

Last night the garden was a-cold,
And we were wrapped in selfish grief,
Today the little garden lies
Warm-covered, leaf by leaf.

The pine tree dropped his needles down
To guard her cherished pansy bed.
To make her foxglove seedlings warm
The maple all his leaves had shed.

With wind and rain and leaf for aid,
From fading to the growing light,
While we forgot, I think that she
Was busy all the night.

Her garden glory safe from harm,
At dawn perhaps, with shining eyes,
A tired, grubby, little ghost
Crept back to Paradise.

LAVENDER

I made my garden borders straight,
Hyacinths on the southern slope,
On either side the little gate
Lemon verbena and heliotrope;
Hollyhocks by the low stone wall,—
(Never a wind but made them stir)
And I said, when the garden slept in fall,
"Next year I shall grow lavender."

'Tis long ago since down the path
Grief walked with June in the garden-plot,
And left behind an aftermath
Of crimson clover and melilot;
I turned me from the garden door,
An exile and a wanderer,
I plucked a leaf and said once more,
"Some day I shall grow lavender."

And so I pray that there may be
Somewhere in heaven a little space
'Twixt shadow and the sun for me
To make again a garden place.
Where, in the cool of twilight air,
(Did they not bring Him gifts of myrrh?)
His blessed feet will stray, and there,
Please God, I shall grow lavender.

OUR GARDEN

It does not bloom under roofs of glass, where the
    air is heavy and languid,
Nor yet in the sheltered valley where the choicest
    fruits have birth,
But high on the sunny uplands where the winds of
    God go over,
Blooms the garden our hands have tended, our
    garden of common earth.

Reflections of glory eternal salute our souls each
    morning,
Our hearts are censers of worship offered up to a
    God above,
Worship compounded of hope and fear and toil the
    sweeter for sharing,
And joy more gentle than passion, and lovelier even
    than love.

On the highroad beyond our garden, the lovers walk
    in their fashion,
Bound for another land than ours, greener valleys
    and clearer skies;
Look me between the eyes, my friends, and clasp my
    hand as a token
We would not change our common earth for all their
    Paradise!

NEW ENGLAND PORT

The tall white houses looking out to sea,
The salty talk of men who somehow knew,
Daylight or dark, what wind it was that blew,
Or how the moon was, what the tide might be.

The shipyard, and a schooner on the ways,
The sound of hammers, the clean smell of pine,
Of tarry cordage, wax, and turpentine,
The beat of gull-wings through the harbor haze.

The sail-loft ruddy in the sunset light,
A great white canvas on the golden floor,
A strong tide pulling steadily off shore,
Workmen's voices calling out good-night.

The land breeze freshening at close of day,
The chuckle of dark water round the piers,
Fog on our faces with the taste of tears,
The lighthouse flashing, fading down the bay.

God's acre, where the mossy headstones keep
The ship in memory with the mariner,
Where marble anchors, carven ropes, occur
Among the crosses and the lambs asleep.

Good to recall now, in another age,
The ships, the men, they made in towns like these.
Their names were mighty upon many seas.
They gave our youth its proudest heritage.

The ships are passing, and the sails are furled.
The deep is lonely for them, and for men
Whose like we shall not look upon again,
Strong men and gentle, in a nobler world.

HOME

May dusk . . . and children calling,
  And the first star.
Slow wreaths of smoke upcurling
  Where little fires are.
A lonely robin singing
  Bravely, boldly, sweet.
Oh, given choice of heaven,
  I think my tired feet
Foregoing pearl and jasper,
  Would find this village street.

Slow wreaths of smoke upcurling
  Where little fires are,
May dusk . . . and children calling,
  And the first star.

HEPATICAS

I had forgotten them, trembling, frail,
Dainty and darling things; not pale
This year of all years but deeper-hued,
Blessing the wood's brown solitude.
Only their fresh grace told me April had blotted
    November.
I had no heart for the spring this year. How then,
    should God remember?

LITTLE ROADS

Gleams of quiet water shining call away
The laggard heart reluctant its weary toil to find.
But when that toil is over, then I shall go some day
And follow all the little roads that I have left behind.

Tangled depths of daisies, bobolinks astir,
Flute-call in the thicket, challenge on the air,
Piney vistas luring, and colored wings a-whirr,
And just beyond the hill-top, Adventure waiting
      there!

Ah the little roadways, far they beckon me
To vagrant gypsy journeys with but a pipe and pack.
Music in the mornings, bread beneath the tree,
And Love alert to greet me some day when I go back!

SONG FOR A LITTLE TOWN

Scornful, cynical phrases,
"Smalltown stuff," "Main Street,"
To me are loved and lovely,
Comforting words, and sweet.

O proud possessive cities,
Ye leave my soul unstirred.
My heart knows but one homeland,
Beloved and absurd.

Main Street. Its green elms arching,
Its river winding down,
Far blue hills rising softly,
My little old home town.

Sorrow and shame may hover
Sinister down that street,
But Love will come following after
On certain and tireless feet.

Engirt with walls of jasper,
I'd never think to rest.
I know a green God's acre,
Where sparrows make their nest.

I'll go again up Main Street,
And there I'll lay me down.
Heaven a far, fair city?
Heaven's a little town.

RETURN TO THE FARM

Here in these fields where death himself has been,
My heart finds help for loneliness and pain
Where trees you planted keep your memory green,
And seed you scattered ripens into grain.

And in the barn's hay-scented, dusky light,
Where gentle beasts awaited gentler friend,
I will remind me of another night,
Another stable, and another journey's end.

MAIN STREET

Under the elms, and the orioles calling
Liquid and clear in the summer sunlight,
Blue river flashing, and bright petals falling,
Never was highway so lovely a sight.

Dear careless fields full of daisies and clover,
Prim little gardens with fragrant brown loam,
Heart's final haven to one lonely rover,
Little town, loved town, your child has come home!

SIGNATURE

While little men revile his name,
And cynics scoff and fools deny,
God seals the year in maple flame,
And scrawls the wild geese on the sky.

ARRIVAL

The forest dark and grim returns
An echo of our wild halloo;
The pebbles slip and slide beneath
The gunwale of our green canoe;
And soon our first camp-fire lifts
A thin smoke-spiral dim and blue.

Across the lake one hermit-thrush
Pours out his soul in promises;
A sudden stir within my heart,
That yesterday could never guess,
Foretells the man that I shall be
When I forsake the wilderness.

PUSSY-WILLOWS

March morning and the robins on the lawn.
A little soft wind calling up the dawn.
A silver sea beneath a golden sky.
A jay's wild yodel clear and high
From out the beeches: then the crash
And clamor of the wrangling crows; a flash
Of swift, divine, uncapturable blue
Across the meadow's barren sombre hue.
A gush of liquid, plaintive melody.
Bluebird come back to home and love and me.

Along the brook spray after precious spray
Of pussywillows pearl and gold and gray.
A chiding call across the pasture lands,
A tired child with treasure-laden hands
Wide-eyed, returning from a magic world.
A dim smoke-pennant drowsily unfurled
Above a roof the drooping boughs just miss.
An open doorway and my mother's kiss.

THE SECRET

My man, he says to me, puzzled like,
"It's wonderful queer," says he,
"When other women are mending socks,
Or gossiping over their tea,
You're lifting your face to the young new moon,
Or calling a bird in a tree,
When other women are mending socks,
Or gossiping over their tea."

I says to my man then, laughing like,
"It's wonderful queer," says I,
"While other men go home to their beds,
And sleep there snug and dry,
You're watching the ships beat down the port,
Or sniffing the winds in the sky,
While other men go home to their beds
And sleep there snug and dry."

My man, he says to me shamefaced like,
"But I'm loving you, lass, the best.
And the wind, and the sea, and the proud clean
    ships,
And the stars our love has blest."
And I kiss my man, and tell him I know,
But I've never told him the rest,
Of that wild bird prisoned in my heart
Till he called it home to his breast.

HOME TREASURE

I have been home to a little house
    In a quiet street in a little town,
There are hills about it, gentle and blue,
    And a silver river winding down.

There's a ship in a green glass bottle set
    On the walnut shelf my father made,
Northern Spies in a China bowl,
    A row of ferns in the stonewall's shade;

There are faded pictures, and rows of books
    Unused, unforgotten, assembled here;
Trophies of school and camp and war,
    Trivial treasure absurd and dear.

Kings go home, I suppose, to palaces,
    And find nothing more precious there
Than a service ribbon, a dog-eared book,
    Or a lock of baby's hair.

WET STREETS

I love wet streets at night;
The long black ways are strung with light;
Gleams of heaped fruit shine through the window-
    mist,
Amber and purple, russet, amethyst.
Under the clustered street-lamps, one by one,
White faces flash and beckon and are gone.
Glimpsed through an open doorway, like a star
Shining down aisles of darkness far and far,—
Within the dim cathedral's towering frame,
Before the altar glows a red, aspiring flame.

ALIEN

The waves mount up, then to the deep returning,
Along the grey rocks, leave a transient stain;
But the tide of my longing surges
And will not ebb again.

Hedge bindweed droops along the heaped grey drift-
    wood
Its frail cups sealed against the bitter rain;
But my heart's full flower opens
And will not close again.

SECRET

God has three hues no painter's brush can capture;
The flush of alder boughs when spring's first rapture
Suffuses them; they are not violet
Nor lavender nor amethyst and yet
Something of each.
         When autumn woods are brave
With their eternal pageant, then God spills
That liquid amber light which He distills
In some divine alembic.
         In His store
Of dyes inimitable God has one more,
The green of grass-blades on a new-made grave.

DICKSONIA AND SWEET-FERN

Dicksonia and sweet-fern! Dicksonia in masses,
Lacey-green and lovely in the spruce-set pasture-
    place,
Down along the stone-wall, swaying in the sunshine,
Deep in its warm caressing depths, you pressed a
    small brown face.

Sweet-fern on the hillside, climbing toward the sky-
    line,
There you stood to glimpse the sea shining blue or
    grey,
Watched the ships go in and out, white and tall and
    stately,
Silver in the dim green pines the sparrows sang all
    day.

Dicksonia and sweet-fern, the gray stone-wall, the
    spruces,
The brown path curving in and out, a very gypsy
    track;
Long ago you left it, but when the world's too weary,
Your heart will find and follow it, and nevermore
    come back!

REQUIESCAT

They buried Shawn Cullinan to-day from the church
    across the street,
The doors of his little shop are closed and its win-
    dows blank and bare;
No more across its threshold stray the shiftless and
    indolent feet
Of the folk, who, frowned on elsewhere, found shel-
    ter and welcome there.

'Twas fifty years ago that he came, gentle and shy
    and young,
With Ireland's wistful courage looking out of his
    clear blue eyes,
His only fortune his Irish faith and an Irish twist to
    his tongue,
And to-day the Mass was said for him—and the tears
    are in our eyes.

There was ever room on the sagging bench set out
    of the summer sun,
Or a nook by the stove in winter for the outcast ones
    of earth;
The loafer, the fool, the pauper, the man whose
    good days were done
Felt his youth, and his hope, and his strength return
    in the sunshine of Shawn's warm mirth.

The child with never a penny to spend found always
    a sweetie to suck,
And trotted off to school or to play with his grimy
    face alight;
The man who shuffled and cleared his throat and
    muttered about his luck,
Took heart at Shawn's gruff, kindly tone, "Come
    in, man, it's all right."

They buried Shawn Cullinan to-day from the church
    across the street,
The wistful Irish eyes are closed, the generous hands
    are still;
The tender heart is pulseless now, and at rest the
    tireless feet,
At rest with the faithful departed in the grave-yard
    on the hill.

It rained to-day while they buried him, but now in
    the twilight, look!
Beyond the tranquil river the west burns clear and
    bright,
And I think when he came to that shining Gate,
    the angel closed his book,
And said in Shawn's own, kindly tone, "Come in,
    Man, it's all right."

BARNEY GLYNN

Sure, of the lads in the place, you're the flower,
You with the sun shinin' out of your eyes,
You with the laugh in your voice spillin' over,
All have a smile for you, witless and wise;

I'm mindin' me now of a day once in April,
Barefoot you came down the dewy bosheen,
Clippin' the heads of the pinky wee daisies,
Under my window you begged a cakeen.

Out of the hawthorn-tree close by the gateway,
Flew a little brown wren, busy-like, in the spring;
Whist! From your hand sped a small wicked pebble
And dead on the sod fell the flutt'rin' wee thing.

Och! The two fists in the blue cryin' eyes of you,
Down fell the dear freckled face on my knee,
And you sobbed, "Make it sing, make it sing again,
        Nora,"
Till I gave you a cake and a sup o' the tea.

I think of that day, when I see the fine shape of you,
Saunterin' still down the same sweet bosheen,
Blarney and coaxin' and smiles for each one of them,
Moira and Bridget and Kate and Eileen.

Ah! Lads are not many and girls, they are plenty,
Only a glance and you'll have your own pick,—
Love go before you and laughter along of you,
God keep an eye on you, Barney avick!

Part Two

MEMORIAL DAY

Veterans were old and tired men,
Who'd fought mysterious battles long ago,
Seven Pines,—Manassas,—and Shiloh,
Who, once a year grew strangely young again,

When through the churchyard gates we watched
them pass,
Absurdly gallant in their dingy blue,
Their old hands shaking as they changed for new
The faded flags above the faded grass.

Moved by a momentary, vague regret,
Sure in your splendid youth, one day you said,
"Whose will be the task, when they are dead,
To wreath the garlands, and the flags to set?"

How traitor time in whom we put our trust
Answers the question that you asked of me!
Incredible that you have come to be
A veteran of foreign wars; your dust

Indifferent, though the brazen bugles play,
Indifferent to the sound of fife and drum,
Unmindful of a last old soldier come
To plant a flag upon your grave to-day.

FOR RAOUL LUFBERRY,

American Ace,

May 19, 1918

A blazing something poised in upper air;
　The sound of guns; the little garden's calm;
The beautiful spent body lying there,
　A stain of scarlet through the idle palm;

Bright ribbons on the boyish breast were burned;
　A gypsy-spirit always at the flame;
Our hero-vagabond, so soon returned
　Into that unknown country whence he came.

His heart be ours!　Let solemn pride prevail
　Through camp and ship and flag-draped aero-
　　drome,
But how our lads in heaven leap to hail
　The prince of all adventurers come home!

NEWS REEL

The great grey ships come proudly up the bay,
  And men in service khaki swing ashore.
Alert and laughing, nonchalant and gay,
  They march along a foreign street once more.

As through our hearts their brothers march again,
  Those other careless boys we used to know,
Who laughed in Metz, and Flanders and Lorraine,
  Only fourteen brief, bitter years ago.

The bright flag flutters softly in the sun
  That glitters back along each bayonet,
O veterans, whose race was early run,
  Trample our traitor hearts, lest we forget

You fought to bring about a lasting peace,
You laid your young lives down that war might
  cease.

PURSUIT

My soul fled shuddering
A terror-ridden thing;
Hot on her heels there came
Poverty, War, and Shame,
Drunkenness, Filth, and Crime,
Innocence fouled with slime,
Unfaith's relentless hounds
Gaining by leaps and bounds,
Passion with scorching breath,
Deformity, Vice, and Death.

Over stubble, grass, and stone,
Fainting, my soul sped on;
Close at her side there stayed
Cheering her steps, a shade,
Impalpable, veiled, and fleet,
Running with tireless feet;
Till the hounds fell back dismayed,
And my soul, no more afraid,
Checking her steps, made bold
To clutch a garment's fold.
Lo! with a sudden grace,
Beauty unveiled her face,
Tender and grave and wise,
Eternity in her eyes!

THE WIRELESS STATION

My soul was sick to surfeit
  With the littleness of things,
Solemn platitudes of men,
  And women's whisperings.

I welcomed in rapt thanksgiving
  The bitter wind from the sea,
Glad of its rough caressing
  And the storm it awoke in me.

Glad of the flash of color,
  Green and violet flame
That leapt into sudden being,
  Crackled and went and came.

In awful, sibilant beauty
  Through conquered,charted air
With the certain rhythm of music,
  And the majesty of prayer.

Till, swept with the great wind's rushing,
  My stubborn heart became
A Pentecostal chamber,
  God in the parted flame!

PARADOX

Not even in remotest Paradise
Can their grim ghosts be tranquil nowadays.
They halt the saints on their appointed ways
Plying them with questions grave and wise.
Galileo turns his troubled eyes
Towards Earth's green glimmer down the starry
    maze,
To English orchards Newton bends his gaze,
Santos-Dumont remembers Rio skies.

Angelo, da Vinci, Edison,—
A host of others: men of mighty wills
Who grieve to see accomplishment undone,
The flocks neglected on a thousand hills,
Sweet harvests lying withered in the sun,
The dusty windows broken in the mills.
      . . .
They saw the Stevensons' tall cones of light
Along the cruel coasts come into flower;
A Quaker stripling caught the lightning's power
The while they watched him through the summer
    night.
To mark the young Lone Eagle on his flight
They sped the breathless cherubim each hour;
When Chrysler set his tools within the tower,
They made no comment but their eyes were bright.

The scars, the sacrifice, the exile's pain,
The laughter of the fools, the freedom banned,
The midnight doubts, forgotten; not in vain,
They said, Watt kept his vigil, Fulton planned,
Bell agonized, that with a silver chain
Of understanding, might the world be spanned.

. . .

Now, scholar, student, genius, priest, and sage,
Proud craftsmen all, they contemplate dismayed
This earth, their lovely workshop disarrayed
By peevish children in their idle rage.
They see us actors on a futile stage,
Or a street rabble routed and betrayed
By vandal leaders weak and renegade,
Unmindful of our princely heritage.

Though winds and floods are harnessed, sea and sky
Are charted to the utmost, secret star,
And deserts Sown, yet impotent we cry:
Saint Michael! All thy portals, screen and bar,
Before our further grovelings they spy,
And the great dead disown us where they are!

ALAN SEEGER

When he swings past with haughty tread,
   All Heaven, I think, must own his thrall
And the dark beauty of that head
   Against the pearl and ivory wall.

With David or with Keats, I guess,
   He deigns a moment to confer,
Chats carelessly with R.L.S.,
   And condescends to Kitchener!

FULFILLMENT

"Oh he's a prince!" The fervent phrase
  Recurs to me now he is dead.
The confident, proud words we said
Of him in college days.

How certainly youth prophesies!
  To-day he holds in fief from God
  Six feet of bitter Flemish sod
And all of Paradise.

HYMN

Every valley has been filled,
Every hill made low.
Through the conquered, charted air
The silver squadrons go.
These, Thy children, ride the storm
Mightier than eagles are,
Where Thy holy highways reach
From Cross to Polar Star.

Men have snared Arcturus' beam,
And walked the ocean floor,
Fashioned fairy webs of steel
Out of stubborn ore.
Swifter than Thy lightning's flash
Science turns a shining key,
Fujiyama's echoes break
Upon Yosemite.

Nations with the nations vie.
In Thy holy sight
All our glories are but toys
Children leave at night.
Lest our treasure with the dawn
Come to be as things abhorred,
Hearken to our prayer, and give
Peace in our time, O Lord!

Melody: Rise My Soul.

NOVEMBER ELEVENTH

A thousand whistles break the bonds of sleep
With swift exultant summons wild and shrill;
Impassioned tongues of flames toward heaven leap
To tell us peace has come. The guns are still.

A thousand flags have blossomed in the air
Like poppies in a garden by the sea.
Beyond the eastern hills a golden flare
Foretells the day that broke on Calvary.

Long-darkened Liberty uplifts once more
Her torch on Belgium, Poland, and Alsace
And Flanders—on each desecrated shore,
Slow dawns the sun; and on my mother's face
The look, I think, that Mary must have worn
In Galilee on Resurrection morn.

DEATH OF A SPORTSMAN

"So this is heaven!," I can hear him say
    And passing Peter with a courteous nod,
    He'll look about to find the throne of God
And be presented in the proper way.

Then having done the right, required thing,
    Gravely he'll quit the presence of the Lord
    And rather lonely and a little bored
Will walk celestial streets, remembering

October stubble, and brown wings a-whir,
    His setters panting in the shade at noon,
    A hard, fast fairway bright with wind and sun;
A motor throbbing and the engine's purr,
    A mountain highway white beneath the moon,
    The clean, green paddock where his ponies run.

APRIL, 1917

Above the grey roofs of the town
A hundred flags against the sky
Flutter and droop and fill again:
The young recruits go marching by
To board the early morning train.

A bugle calls across the crowd.
The Band swings down the trodden way
With Boy-Scouts khaki-clad and lean,
And conscious school-girls prim and proud;
And darting urchins mad with glee,
And motor-cars with banners gay.
'Tis crashing music, colour, life,
And stirring drum and startling fife,
Young lips that cheer, young eyes that dance,
Adventure, glory, and romance.

Babble of voices, bits of song,
A warning whistle down the track,
A thrill electric through the throng,
The band blares into ecstasy.
Aloof and still in dingy black
A woman tells her rosary.

FIRST TO FALL

I cannot think of you among the immortals,
One of a grave-eyed, reverential host;
I picture you come back, a gallant ghost
To seek again these stately, shadowy portals
And hide your khaki 'neath a scholar's gown.
I can imagine how your face will lighten
When you behold against the western sky,

Brilliant and bold, the service banners fly,
And one by one the frat house windows brighten
Above the river as the sun goes down.

Then sauntering down the chapel aisle you go,
Insouciant, indifferent, and slow,
A sidelong glance of mingled pride and shame
For the bright tablet that will bear your name.

TREES OF PICARDY

Now April turns my orchard boughs
To rose and snow along the lane;
Last year, they say, the stricken trees
Knowing they might not bloom again,
Were ruddier and lovelier
In Alsace and Lorraine.

A monarch at the garden gate,
My maple rears a kingly head;
This year on Ypres' scarlet sod
A sapling maple grove burns red;
Canada's little exile trees
Above her exile dead.

Beyond our river's placid rim
The poplars whisper secretly.
How can you welcome spring again
Next year, and all the years to be,
But to be hewn for crosses new,
O trees of Picardy?

My poplars bend their boughs to me
And say, "We stood on Calvary."

BACK HOME

With deep unfathomable eyes
Fixed on the fire; with eager ears
And drooping crest, his setter lies
And waits the step he never hears.

November night is starry cool.
The firelight plays on book and chair,
On needles thrust in soft brown wool,
And on her softly-shining hair.

Under her breath his mother sings
As to and fro her needle flies.
And all she knits are soldier things
And all her songs are lullabies.

FOR A CANTONMENT LIBRARY

With a copy of Stewart Edward White's "The Forest"

Go, little book, and bring to him,
The soldier-lad who reads you through:
The sight of pine-woods massed and dim,
The scent of wood-smoke curling blue:
The sound of rain upon the tent,
The sense of peace that comes to all
Who love God's house of out-of-doors,
And answer when the Red Gods call.

Go, little book, and promise him
Who holds you in his hand to-day:
His feet shall know again those trails
He trod, content, but yesterday;
He shall lie down again to sleep
In cleaner camps, by clearer streams,
When Peace comes back to bide with us,
And God restores to us our dreams.

IN AN OLD GRAVEYARD

All in their narrow graves they lie,
Life and its flurry past and done.
While at the gate, Forsythia
Shakes out her golden branches in the sun.

Low mossed headstones and shadows deep,
Soft April winds that whispering pass
And finger with caressing touch
Faded flags above the faded grass.

While overseas, in Flanders Field,
Where clear the little rivers run,
Dust that once was flesh I loved,
Blossoms in the sun.

THE PARADOX

"She is a nation bestial in her hate,
A nation blind to beauty's pure appeal;
She sees the world in bloody chaos reel,
And bares her teeth in rage insatiate.
She said, 'Let there be darkness. Desecrate
Ocean and earth and sky with flame and steel.
My might is right. Let war's red mist conceal
The helpless hands that stretch importunate'."

These be the bitter words our lips have learned;
But what of him—that lithe, high-hearted lad,
Who made our golden college days more glad?
And what of him whose wise old heart so yearned
Over the heedless youths beneath his care?
Her sons they are, who fight for her, somewhere.

A PRAYER

For the strong hands, Lord,
And the resolute and sure,
For the will that understands,
And the strength that can endure.

For the soul serene to bear
What of ill the years afford,
For the impulse straight and fair,
And the white heart, Lord!

"UNFIT FOR SERVICE"

Next June Alumni Field will glow again
With all its old Commencement coloring.
And from the college pines the whitethroats sing
Just as of old in immemorial pain.
And men will praise their deeds who cleansed from
     stain
War's desecrated fields that they might bring
Their laurels to thy feet, so honoring
Themselves and thee, O Alma Mater Maine!

I think of him whom fate would not allow
The bugle and the khaki and the gun;
His unrecorded battle quickly done,
He sits a bit aloof in heaven now,
Applauding when his brothers picture how
Argonne, Belleau, or Epernay was won.

YALE CAMPUS
(*1917*)

September lights again her leafy fires.
Scarlet on somber stone the woodbine clings.
The Sparrows chirp and flutter in the wires,
The walls are patterned with leaf-flickerings
And shadows of the sparrow wings.

Long gleaming columns blot the peaceful view.
And little gold leaves blowing off the trees
Fleck transiently the khaki and the blue
And brush caressingly the cheeks of these,
Who hold in their young hands old destinies.

When these your children, Yale, war-worn and hard
In spirit and in flesh come back again,
God grant they leave behind as fair a sward,
As sunny and as safe and sweet from stain,
In Picardy and Flanders and Lorraine.

AMENDE

I swore in my youth a boastful word,
"For no man's sake will I bear a sword."
Thy henchmen stormed my castle, Lord.

Now in thy service must I go
All unhardened against the foe.
Soldier and Master, canst thou know?

How as I mount where thy standard leads,
Or stumble whither thy charger speeds,
Under its mail my body bleeds.

The sword that would serve thee, Captain, King,
Wavers as I stand sickening,
And turns in my hand like a living thing.

Till my spent heart rallies my body, "Now
What of thy youth and its braggart vow?
Coward and trickster and weakling,—thou?"

Send me not from thy ranks away,
Nor bid me from the battle stay,
Grant me no mercy, this I pray.

Be thy face for me an iron mask,
Choose for my doing the bloodiest task,
This be the mercy, Lord, I ask.

Till over my wounds the flesh has grown,
Then, naked, joyous, and alone,
I shall face thy foemen and atone.

I swore in my youth a boastful word,
Now I ha' done with boasting, Lord.
When my hands are scarred, I shall need no sword.

OUT OF THE DARK

Dedicated to Rudy Vallee

Out of the dark a clear young voice,
   Into our hearts an old refrain,
And we say to our small sons, "Listen!"
   As we come to our feet, "for Maine."

Our friends may smile at the gesture
   But somehow we cannot say
That our hearts are back on the campus
   With our brothers of yesterday.

With the men who were younger, and weaker,
   And wiser, and stronger, than we,
Who were surer and saner and bolder,—
   The men that we used to be.

There's a hush over blue Stillwater,
   The lights gleam gold on the snow,
The brothers are singing together
   Along Fraternity Row.

76

"Fill the steins to dear old Maine,
   Shout till the rafters ring,—"
Shoulder to shoulder at twilight
   They gather together and sing,

So hearing, our hearts remember,
   And that one voice wakens again
Gallant and ghostly visions
   Of men who died for Maine.

Only the twirl of a dial,
   The click of a switch, but Hark!
Are you listening in, my brothers,
   Out in the outermost dark?

BROADCAST

Last year we stood together at this hour
Above the tumult of the Avenue,
And thrilled with wonder, from a giant tower,
We sent a Christmas message out to you.

We visioned past far snow-swept forest places,
Your cabin, and your fire's lonely flame.
Aurora painting all the sky's blue spaces,
A dial turning.   Quiet.   Then your name

And "Merry Christmas."   For we found you, found
        you,
Despite the distance and the trackless dark,
And for a moment then, our arms were round you.
It's Christmas Eve again to-night, and hark!

Still farther distance, deeper dark defeating,
Certain that you will listen in and hear,
Relayed from star to star we send our greeting,
"A Merry Christmas, and A Glad New Year."

"AND IT IS NOT WELL TO TARRY
AT THE GODS' FEAST"—

The Odyssey. Book III

Long since our brethren turned to arms. And long
  Insatiate monsters worked their hidden will.
Each hour the wine-dark sea grew darker still
With kindred blood to feed a kindred wrong,
While we beguiled the time with feast and song,
  What cared we, while we ate and drank our fill?
  Within our hearts no sacrificial thrill.
What cared we, if we might our peace prolong?

The dusk comes on. Far off the gods retreat.
  The night with menacing is all beset.
A whisper comes to each: "It is not meet
To linger at such banquets. Ah, be fleet
  And pour libation ere the dawn be met.
  The gods are mighty. Pray the gods forget."

80

NOSTALGIA

A drift of snowflakes pure and cold,
The happy theatre-going crowd,
The trolleys, moving blots of gold,
The painted ladies furred and proud;
A gypsy girl in gaudy rags,
The taxis' raucous tremolo,
The softly-blowing Allied flags
A thousand, thousand lights aglow;
The mystery-enshrouded park,
Tall spires soaring to the blue.
O city smiling in the dark,
How lovely and how luring you!

Then, clanging down the autumn sky
From far cloud-cities falling,
That strident summons hoarse and high,
Of wild geese calling, calling!

Part Three

LAD

What you were to me, Lad,
  That you'll never guess,
Your strength a shelter from the storm,
  A cloak of tenderness.
With you my heart has found those shores
  To which all hearts aspire,
Bohemia, Acadia,
  The Land of Heart's Desire.

What you are to me, Lad,
  That you'll never know;
With you I walk the path erstwhile
  I never hoped to go.
All the lost heroes of romance
  Smile from your eyes, my lad,
Lancelot and Lionheart,
  Blondel and Galahad.

What you'll be to me, Lad,
  That you'll never dream.
With you my vision finds again
  The glory and the gleam.
The goals for which all souls must strive
  Loom for me where you are,
At once the harbor and the deep,
  The morrow and the star!

PROFESSION

All things serve you: lights at nightfall,
Brown old roads that lure to follow,
Children flushed with sleep or laughter,
Hill-mist in a purple hollow,
Sails against a dim horizon,
Whistled music; the first star,
All that makes life quick and lovely,
Sends my heart to where you are.

Seagulls flashing; swift cloud shadows
Over stubble hillsides trailing,
Masts that rock beyond the house-tops,
Docks and wharves; longshoremen hailing;
Scream of engines through the darkness,
Forms and faces strange of hue,
All that wakes the urge to wander,
Brings me back again to you.

Scarlet maples; smoky asters,
First soft snow at twilight falling,
Open water sealed with silver,
Empty gardens; wild geese calling;
Dead leaves drifted down the highroad,
Early darkness; candle-glow;
All that hints of home and shelter,
Bids me follow where you go.

Love, I dare believe that beauty
Kindles with her every breath
Torches that will light me to you
Past the shadowed gates of death.

DISCOVERY

Five white sails far out on the sky-line,
Over the grey sun-smitten rock, the shadow of sea-
  gull wings,
Buttercup gold and purple of iris
Vivid against the gnarled green pine, where a spar-
  row sings and sings;
Straight o'er the sea a path of silver
Shimmering clear to the Happy Isles where the
  crimson sun drops low,
Somewhere a tern is calling, calling,
Lad that I never loved at all, it's you I'm wanting so!

DE PROFUNDIS

I have seen a great wave born at sea,
Hollow emerald curve and crystal spray,
Destined to hurl its splendor far away
Upon some cloistered northern shingle where
Song-sparrows call all day.

Sparrow songs were chimes that marked my days,
My life that quiet seabeach set apart,
Lacking love's rapture, yea, but love's keen smart,
Until God urged your splendid passion home
To break upon my heart.

ARRAIGNMENT

From love and love's tumult I dwelt apart.
Men thought me wise and gentle and controlled,
Even, perhaps they said, a little cold,
You laid your naked hands along my heart.

And all the peace I cherished yesterday
Is vanished down the darkling way you came,
Flame in your glance and on your lips a flame,
Joy is a bauble I have thrown away.

My days go by in hypocritic guise.
A shameless creature waiting for your kiss,
A lawless girl who recks no hour but this,
Looks back at me with strange and hostile eyes.

Another self has risen in my stead.
I would to God that she, or I, were dead!

CARPE NOCTEM

Love me to-night. Outside the storm
   Beats at our citadel in vain,
Herein is warmth and harmony
   And peace from pain.

Love me to-night. For with the dawn
   On diverse ways our feet must fare,—
  You to your own old world, and I
   To God knows where.

Ah, leave the window. Turn to me
   And read my willing lips aright.
Remember,—or forget this hour,—
   Love me to-night.

AFTER STORM

A world new-washed with silver
    And drenched in mystery,
And grey mist lifting, drifting, drifting,
    Ah, whitethroat, sing to me!

The riot of wet roses,
    June roses sweet with rain,—
And then the whitethroat calling, calling,
    Ah, Dear, your lips again!

CONFESSION

Gay, gentle, valiant (I was none of these)
  And generous, you called me, strong and wise.
'Twas only that glad youth danced in my eyes
As dances April wind through young green trees.
It was so easy then to charm and please
  For you were swift to praise, loath to advise,
  Slow to condemn, and quick to sympathize,
Humility has brought me to my knees.

My heart was virgin soil. You dreamed and planned
  A garden fit to welcome feet divine.
  But O my very dear, not yours or mine,
Its few and futile flowers to command.
Fate plucks them with a rude and random hand,
  They wither at a desecrated shrine.

GREETING

Somebody mentioned your name last night,
In the casual way people do,
When they talk of old days, and old plays, and old
    ways,
But it made me homesick for you!
Your path may lead to the far Southern Cross,
And mine to the green Northern Star,
But distances end, when friend says to friend,
"God bless you, wherever you are!"

THE WOODS ROAD

Ah, choose some other path, when next you go
Across the green God's country which we know.
There must be many roads besides that one
Bronze in the shadow, silver in the sun.
For, oh my very dear, it seems to me,
If you should walk that way, mysteriously
My heart would know.   And should you smile
Into another's eyes, and all the while
The whitethroats called unheeded,—for their sake,
Across a thousand miles, my heart would hear,—
    and break!

FULFILLMENT

He would open for her, she dreamed,
  In some intimate, sacred hour,
His inviolate treasures of memory,
  And their glory should be her dower,—
All his child's far concept of fame to be,
  All his boyhood's dim vision of power.

He has shown her his memories
  In the dusk where they must abide.
There's no vision of power, no shadow of fame,
  But her longing is satisfied.
For she knows of his buccaneer cave in the woods,
  And his little dog that died.

PERVERSE

My heart, you said, was a garden,
You would pluck its flowers, unheeding,—
Roses snow-white, and gold, and red,—
Lover, your hands are bleeding!

HOME-COMING

We should have loved each other long ago
  Before your heart became a trysting-street,
  Where old ghosts congregate on furtive feet,
In April when barbaric tulips blow.

Before you learned the sudden overthrow
  Of my hard-won contentment at the beat
  Of old, unhappy music bittersweet
With memories you cannot share or know.

But faint and frail youth's gaudy flowers show
  Beside the garden that we plan next year.
  How trivial all music when I hear
At dusk, your silver, whistled tremolo,
  Your happy step, your whispered, "Ah, my dear,
We should have loved each other long ago!"

THE BETTER PART

To you, love is a cloak;
  Within its fold,
Your heart is guarded safe
  From storm and cold.

Love is the storm to me;
  From farthest North
Its bitter winds arise
  And hale me forth.

Love is to you a shield
  Unmarred by strife;
Across its shining rim,
  You look on life.

Love is a sword to me;
  With my last breath,
I'll kiss the bloody hilt
  And smile at death.

Love is a rose to you,
  Of passion born;
I pass the flower by,
  And choose the thorn.

The cloak will drop away,
Rust stain the shield;
The rose to summer sun
Or wind, must yield.

At Time, their conqueror,
I smile in scorn;
He but makes sharp for me
Storm, sword, and thorn.

THE SNAPSHOT

Once, just once, Lad, look as if you loved me,
Lift that splendid shapely head and smile into my
  eyes,
Sun and shade, conspire with me to snare this
  radiant moment,
Lips, give back the banter my frozen heart denies.

Another year the orioles will flash along Stillwater,
Tulips flame on all the lawns, barbaric red and gold,
Other feet will find these trails, linger by our river,
Tell me, Lord, how shall I learn to bear it, growing
  old?

Once, just once, Lad, look as if you loved me,
(Gay good-byes tomorrow, Heart, not a hint of
  tears!)
Just a kodak picture, a piece of printed paper,
Out of all youth's wanton spoil, to cheat the barren
  years!

"I HAVE NO WISH TO CLAIM
YOUR LOVE . . . "

I have no wish to claim your love, and yet
   I cannot quite relinquish thought of claim.
That quick wild thrill at mention of your name
The flesh will not forego nor blood forget.
Be free of me. Find new love, nor regret
   The hazard of the gods. Be theirs the blame
   Who grant that alien hands may tend the flame
That leapt upon their altars when we met.

I saw a woman once who gave her child
   To those who swore to love it as their own.
Her voice was gentle and her gesture mild.
   She kissed its cheek and went away alone.
But I could guess, although she gave no sign,
The voice that clamored in her heart, "Mine!
   Mine!"

APRIL TIDE

Out of a mesh of tangled, bare elm-branches,
The moon emerges.
Below, against the rocks in liquid silver,
The ocean surges.
The moon would lull the world,
The sea would wake it,
And both would break the heart,
Could beauty break it.

A year ago, in confidence undying,
We two together,
Beheld the world grow magical with moonrise
And April weather.
"In Time's gray ash," you said,
"Will shine Love's embers."
Tell me, O Moon and Sea, that he
Somewhere, remembers!

REMINDER

Where my garden used to be,
Year after year, one daffodil
Returns to laugh a little while.
So though my mind knows naught of you,
Somehow the sudden thought of you
Is like the flower's smile.

THE "IMITATIONS"

This is the little book he loved
  When he loved me; the book
We read together in those quiet ways
  He long ago forsook.

These are his markings, growing dim,
  But ineffaceable upon my heart
As is the constant thought of him,
  Though we are years apart.

This is the little book he loved,
  When he loved me. I pray
Dear God, no favour in his thought
  All through his unknown day.

But when night comes and his strong soul
  Reveals itself to Thee,
In his prayers, too, I wonder, Lord,
  Has he forgotten me?

EYES THAT HAVE HELD MY HEAVEN . . .

Eyes that have held my heaven in their depths
Hold it no more. And eager lips
That kindled passion to the soul's eclipse
Grow cold on mine. Impetuous hands
Could twist my heart with rapture or despair.
Not now. "I have grown peaceful as old age."
Ecstasy and terror and heartbreak
Are little letters on a printed page.
I dream no more. Nor do I weep.
Day brings a task.
And night brings sleep.

Hope cannot rouse me any more.
Life is a toy I have grown weary of.
Its grief as futile as the thing called love.
From what deep source then, comes this wild delight,
That daily I am shaken to the core
Until my quickened soul towards joy takes flight,
Because of jasmin . . . the keen kiss of spray . . .
A dead man singing *Eurydice?*

CHALLENGE

Somebody whistles clearly down the street
And Chloe hears and fails to turn the page.
The mockingbird repeats it from his cage,
The jasmine floods the room with odors sweet.

Shy wings are stirring in the cedar hedge,
Wild bird the prisoned bird would greet.
Somebody whistles clearly down the street.
The jasmine branches tap the window ledge.

Its blossoms flood the room with odors sweet.
The elders talk of divers dreary things:
Of deaths and wars and maids and marketings,—
Somebody whistles clearly down the street.

So Time flings down to Youth the gage,
In Life's grim lists his certain fate to meet;
Somebody whistles clearly down the street,
And Chloe hears . . . and fails to turn the page.

QUESTION

Someone tries across the court
To play the Traumerei,
One of the things we never heard
Too often, you and I,
Down in our little bright café
Back in those days ere love was dead.
What were those lines you liked to say,
Of "Music more than music,
And bread . . . not only bread?"

The Dream-song ends. Old wonder wakes
And unforgotten longings leap;
If love can die, how will God keep
The promise that all music makes?

A HAWAIIAN RECORD

Brown bodies shining on the golden sand,
  Three scarlet poppies shaken by the gale,
White foam blown backward from a great green
        wave,
  Far out where sea and sky-line meet,—a sail . . .

Sunlight and sky and sea,
  Song to the heart's desire,
Song that bids the spirit sleep,
  And wakes the flesh to fire!

HER RING

Now and again the sunlight
Reveals the stone's white fire
And the colors leap and struggle
Like laughter and desire.

The jewel for a moment
Can call my thought apart;
But forever and forever
Her slim hands hold my heart.

THIRST

"I know a place," you said to me to-day,
"In Murch's pasture, where a little pool
Widens beneath the gnarled and murmuring pines.
The stream runs deep there. It is dark and cool
And quiet, yet the spot is somehow gay
With bright pipsissewa and partridge vines.
You'll always hear at twilight the same bird
Singing now near, now very far away.
The moss is green as green along the brink
And soft as soft. The ferns shoulder-high . . ."

Then you fell silent with no other word.
But underneath your speech I heard a cry
Ancient as exile and as desperate,
As old as Judah and Jerusalem:
The cry of David pressed by Philistines,—
"Oh that one would give me but to drink
The water of the well of Bethlehem
Which is beside the gate!"

I saw a look they knew in David's eyes,
Those three strong men who went in jeopardy.
I saw the gnarled pine-branches lift and swing
Sharply green against familiar skies;
I smelled the brown brook, and the ferns that sway,
Tumble and tilt, each on its angled stem,

110

I heard the thrushes chiming lone and late
And felt a little wind begin to stir,
That little sunset wind that seems to bring
His own hearth-smoke unto the wanderer.

And guessed within your heart what waters poured
Like David's on the ground before the Lord.

HOUSE O'DREAMS

There'll be a path among the pines
To a secret place I know;
And hollyhocks in nodding lines
When I build my bungalow,

A broad stone step, an open door,
And a glimpse of garden through,
Beyond the garden a hint of moor
And the far hills high and blue;

A long low room with shelves of books
And pictures two or three,
And an eastern window niche that looks
Toward a silver strip of sea.

A red brick hearthway glowing bright
With birchen limb on limb,
And in your eyes, my dear, the light
That makes all fires dim!

THE PROVENCAL SPEAKS

My love goes walking lonely
  Somewhere there in the South.
Stain of the sun on her slim forearm,
  And berry-stain on her mouth.

Trenches and towns will vanish,
  Travail and terror and pain,
When my love's brown hands shall cleanse me
  And make me whole again.

Shattered the might of my manhood,
  And the glory of my youth.
But Fate I forgive 'gin I kiss again
  The berry-stain from her mouth.

INTERVAL

When spring returns to walk these ways again,
To stain far hills with deeper violet,
To veil the hollow where two roads are met,
And shake the shadbush out in every lane;

When whitethroats voice the immemorial pain
Of exile,—cancelled all your exile's debt,
You will forsake (you would not quite forget)
The Southern Cross below the Spanish Main.

Your soldier heart will leap when dawns in view
That soft French shore where sternest days begin;
But first I ask of God—not as my due—
(Since any thought of self now ranks as sin)
But of His grace,—one little hour with you
On some clean sea-beach when the tide comes in.

NIGHT CLUB

Perhaps you'll call me at the close of day,
   When all the Park is grey with winter rain.
   You will assail my silence all in vain.
"He does not answer," so a voice will say.

I shall have checked my garment at a door,
   And shown the card, as patrons recommend;
   I am assured that many a long-lost friend
Will greet me as I cross the shining floor.

There'll be old wine to drink, old tales to tell,
   Even, who knows?—a window whence we'll mark
   Swung far below us in a misty arc
This, our city, we have loved so well.

And there I'll find a table laid for two,
Where I shall sit content and wait for you.

SONG

Tonight a cloud is blown across the moon,
  And Psyche's lifted lips are like a rose
That offers to the wind its fragrant boon.
  Whom Psyche loves tomorrow, no one knows.

Whom Psyche loves tomorrow no one knows.
  Tonight a cloud is blown across the moon;
Tonight the wandering winds caress a rose,
  Tomorrow and the sunlight come too soon.

Tonight her lifted lips are like a rose,
  Tomorrow and the sunlight come too soon.
Whom Psyche loves tomorrow, no one knows;
  But ah tonight! that cloud across the moon!

TO COPHETUA'S BEGGAR MAID

Dear, when the king stepped down
Splendid in robe and crown,
And laid on your tanned young arm
His slender nerveless palm,
Bidding you stay and be
Queen o'er his kingdoms three,
Promising shelter and ease,
Jewels and broideries,
Dear, did you think of these . . .

The dim green woods forsaken,
The far faint trails not taken,
The village roads that wind away silver in the sun,
The pool below the meadow
Enclosed in alder shadow,
And how the thrushes sing there when the summer
    day is done?

Queen, when the king grows old,
Queen, when his love grows cold,
Gems on your fingers white
Will show as fair a light;
As dainty and as sweet
Your bread, your wine, your meat,
As soft your rugs, and yet
When day and dusk are met,
Beggar, can you forget . . .

While great cloud-ships go over,
The wind that lifts the clover
And runs impalpable and fleet across the golden
  grain,
The blackbirds mad and merry,
The hill, the forge, the ferry,
And a slender, swarthy vagabond whose eyes are
  dark with pain?

TO A REALIST

Life is a prison, friend of mine, you say?
No, nor a palace, but, friend, yesterday
Life was a little house but garnished fine and fair,
Set by the roadside free to sun and air.
The road was dusty, yea, but it was sweet,
Checkered by sun and shade and safe for childish
    feet.
Now swept by storms and gusts of bitter rain
Dark is our road; it will be light again
And God in His good time obliterate our pain.

SIXTEEN

"Good-night," my father says and winds the clock.
My mother smooths her work and lays it down
And puts the thread and thimble in their place.
She folds my father's paper. "Coming, Ned,"
She calls to him and then she lifts my face
And kisses me. "Good-night, my dear," she says.
I close my book and go upstairs to bed.

A little sweet wind makes my curtains sway,
A bar of moonlight lies along the spread.

Across the hall I hear low voices say,
"I 'phoned about the roof;" "The gas-bill came
        to-day."
The baby stirs and whimpers fretfully
And Mother comforts him, "Sh, sh, my dear."
She croons; then whispers from my doorway, "Jean,
You're warm enough? How bright the moon is here!
Good-night." A door shuts. Then the clock strikes
        ten
And everyone is fast asleep but me.

A motor-car purrs by and stops. I hear
Low laughter from the little house next door.
Then comes a pause, and though I cannot see,
I know someone has just been kissed. And soon,
"Good-night," again. The motor glides away.
Somebody whistles clearly down the street.
I lie here in my room that's bright as day,
My body white and still beneath the sheet,
My heart a mad thing underneath the moon!

TO R.L.S.

Comrade, we of the brotherhood, summon your soul,
    out yonder,
We who await the foe with weaponless hands and
    frail,
We who have felt the exile's rain cleaving our hearts
    asunder,
Whom the White Plague has smitten, give you our
    dauntless hail!

Yea, and we give you thanks for the music of chil-
    dren's laughter,
And the flash of a bonny sword in the thick of a
    loyal fight,
And the sight of a pirate ship with death before
    and after,
All the life of the dear world shining in the darkness
    of our night.

Because you trod the way, our feet have learned to
    love it,
The road is never silent, for your singing echoes
    still;
And the path is never steep, since we behold, above
    it,
A lone grave looking seaward, upon Vailima's hill.

Heartened, we turn away from the altar of your
      spirit,
Your prayer, so nobly granted, our lips repeat again;
And your command,—O Captain, how we lift our
      hearts to hear it,
In the Valley of the Shadow, make us men!

IN PRAISE OF OLD LADIES

I love old ladies: soft white hair,
And tender, wrinkled hands that care
For tired men; caressing words
For little, helpless things,—small birds
And children; sweet, incisive speech,
And gentle silences that teach
Serenity and kindliness,
And faith in ancient promises.

I love their unregretful praise
Of other, simpler days and ways,
Of scenes that old songs bring to mind.
I marvel at their power to find
New truth in homely, hackneyed phrase.
I love their dear and dainty ways,
Their reminiscent tears and smiles
In sunny kitchens and church aisles.

But most of all I love old eyes
Not too intent on Paradise,
Eyes that have found the long years good,
Eyes that have asked and understood.
Dear God, when I at last grow old,
Grant that my life may likewise hold
Martha's care for each small thing,
And Mary's serene listening.

REAGENT

As in the chemist's sterile graduate,
A single element of potent strength
Clouds, obscures, diffuses, and at length
Resolves into a bright precipitate;
So in the tranquil liquid of my life
The acid of pain wrought by treachery
Diffuses, darkens, clears, until I see
Beauty in all elemental strife,
That simple, savage creed my fathers knew.
Who asked no abstract heaven for their due,
From death no retribution life denied.
With these strong foods their mouths were
    satisfied,
Ah would to God that I might taste them too,
Revenge and passion, tyranny and pride!

MY BOYS

"But we are all candles in the wind." Meredith.

I taught them from the sober height of years
    Term after term, my academic lore;
But they, within a frenzied twelvemonth's span,
    Have taught me more.

I saw them as that Master-Spirit saw
    Mankind: each soul an upward-reaching fire
But blown about by little winds of youth
    And youth's desire.

The mightiest wind that ever shook this world
    (Loud at our very doors we hear it beat!)
But blows their souls to white and steady flame
    About God's feet.

AN ODE FOR THE DIAMOND JUBILEE
OF MOUNT DE CHANTAL

Three score and fifteen years ago,
God planted a garden here,
When He sent to these placid meadow lands,
Like a brood of doves, His gentle nuns
With the seed of Faith in their hands.

Storms beat on the tiny garden,
Assaulting its fragile wall;
Winds battered about its portals
Till they threatened to fail and fall;
But I think God found the garden dear
For hope made a sturdy fence about,
And love was a hedge to keep hate out,
And Faith bloomed all the year.

Joy flamed soon in its borders,
For nuns have a magic touch.
Peace appeared, a flowering tree,
Grace was a vine that clung to trust;
Wisdom flourished with courtesy
Close to the lily of modesty
Our Lady loves so much.
Children came in their tender youth
To gather the fragrant store.
Hope made a wreath about their feet
And love lured them back with its odors sweet,
To Mount de Chantal's door.

Some found the narrow paths more sweet,
And the world outside less dear.
So, moved, somehow, with a strength divine,
They wove a garland of hope and love,
And said, as they laid their lives at a shrine,
"Lady, our hearts bide here."

To-day in joy and splendor,
The garden is aflame.
And her children gather from far and near,
For the glory of her name;
And they sing her praise and her length of days,
And Mount de Chantal's fame.

Mystical Rose, look down on our garden,
Let the winds blow lightly over this place,
Guard all the blossoms thy hand-maidens tend.
Turn the storm aside, and, we pray thee, send
The sunlight of thy face.
Till the world is a dream and time a wraith,
Guard thou unsullied to the end,
The flower of our Faith!

MY WISH

If I could be who I would be,
If suddenly to me God said,
"Of all my dear and noble dead
Choose one to be again on earth
For strife or service, toil or mirth,
Resume, one hour, mortality,—"
I know right well who I would be.

If I could go where I would go,
In all the lovely lands that are
From Southern Cross to Polar Star,
If I could linger for a space
In one long-loved, earth-hallowed place,
Why, then God's will should set me down
At nightfall in a Scottish town.

In "Leerie's" shape I would go forth
Through that dim city of the North,
And run again with eager feet
Along the Edinboro' street,
To light the gas lamps, one by one,
And nod to little Stevenson!
And as he lay in bed, he'd see
My street-stars shining in a row.

If I could be who I would be,
If I could go where I would go.

ASPIRATIONS

Oh for open water,
The swoop and scream of seagulls,
The salt wind's fierce caressing,
The smell of pine and tar;
The creak of sails slow lifting,
The sight of masts and cordage,
Of ships come into harbor
And schooners plying far;
The surge and shock of billows,
The sheen of charging graybacks,
And out beyond the seawall,
A slanting carmine spar.

The beat of sturdy engines
That throb all night in darkness
And find their hidden havens
To rock at dawn in ease;
The sense of bonds unshackled,
A soul set free to journey,
A ship whose canvas flutters
With every vagrant breeze;
All time's old griefs would vanish,
Tomorrow's glory beckon,
Oh for open water,
And a heart bound overseas!

FRIENDS

When others fail, forsake, forget,
Two friends I have who greet me yet.

The one a pagan creature is
Bare to the sun's exultant kiss,
The rain's caress upon her breast;
The crawling, crowded earth she spurns,
Halloos the stars to heel, and turns
Her body at the wind's behest.

And one loves children, sheep that go
Slow-cropping, twilight, candle glow,—
Yet grips a horse between her knees,
And flashes high a naked blade,
And dreams of white roads in the shade
Of little, whispering poplar trees.

O Beauty! swift to heal and bless
The heart assailed with loneliness.
Daily you summon me to mark
Serene above the city's fret,
These gracious friends who greet me yet,
Diana and the young Jeanne d'Arc!

NOCTURNE

A lonely wind is wandering down the world,
A bird cries somewhere and will not be still;
The banners of the summertime are furled,
Her green tents folded far by hedge and hill.

Come, play to me, and as the twilight closes,
Let us forget the cry which will not cease.
Let us have firelight, perfume of roses,
The sound of music and the sense of peace.

Herein is shelter, home, the love of friends,
And youth was with us only yesterday;
Beside this hearthstone all desire ends,
Content comes in to bide with us alway.

The swollen river floods the sombre meadows,
The fire fades,—grey ash and sodden spark;
A lonely wind goes seeking through the shadows,
Ah God! That wild bird calling in the dark!

MY GRAVE

I know the place my grave will be,
A low green slope with tossing clover near
Where I shall lie all June and smile to hear
The bobolinks' mad music over me.

COMPANIONSHIP

I love to find upon a random page
Beside some true and lovely line,
Yellowed perhaps, or grown quite faint with age
A marking fine,
Like a friend's hand on mine.

Or when I go as dusk and daylight meet,
Out from the noisy city ways
To light a candle at Our Lady's feet,
And tell her praise,
To find them all ablaze.

Wherefore I lift my heart in joy and prayer,
That of his grace God condescends
To greet me all along life's thoroughfare
Until it ends,
With goodly, ghostly friends.

BEAUTY OF YOUTH

Beauty of childhood's dawn,—pink palms and warm,
    clinging fingers,
Beauty of motherhood, the worn, wan face bent
    nearer,
Beauty of tranquil age when death stands loath in
    the shadow,
Dear are these beauties, O Lord, but the beauty of
    youth is dearer.

Beauty of flames in the dark, secret, insatiate, laugh-
    ing,
Beauty of whirling green waters enduring ice-fetters
    no longer,
Beauty of hollow-mouthed winds unleashed on the
    limitless prairie,
Strong are these beauties, O Lord, but the beauty
    of youth is stronger.

Beauty of wayside shrines untouched by war's de-
    vastation,
Beauty of sudden music hallowing swiftly or slowly,
Beauty of hushed cathedrals, faith a palpable pres-
    ence,
Holy these beauties, O Lord, but the beauty of
    youth is more holy.

Beauty of great achievement, beauty of love triumphant,
Beauty of splendid sacrifice, beauty of utter truth,
Beauty of deaths heroic, beauty of laugh-borne
bondage,
These were enough to vision Thee, but, Lord, the
beauty of youth!

FIREFLIES

Fireflies glimmer and glow and gleam.
Each is a sudden and magical spark.
And I like to think that somebody's dream
Blossoms, out there in the dark!

NEXT DOOR

Often I wake at night and hear
Tread of hoofs on the stable floor,
And I know that Doctor John next door
Is up and off through wind and rain
To a lighted room, where Hope and Fear
Clasp hands across the bed of Pain.
And I say a little prayer and then
Drift off to quiet sleep again.

CLOSING

The hour for their nightly turn arrives.
   She stands erect before a narrow board
   And fits her body to a marking scored
Deeper and deeper by a thousand knives.

Then, deft and casual, her partner drives
   Each quick, accustomed dagger swiftly toward
   Her rigid form. Unnoted, unencored,
They bow. The curtain drops across their lives.

How long, she wonders, as the bright blades hiss
   And thud about her flesh in lines of steel,
   How long before her taunting heart will feel
In its warm core, their icy, ultimate kiss?

He will be smiling as he turns to go
Content at last that he has stopped the show.

INTO THE NIGHT

A boat puts out from shore
  Into the unknown night;
Daring the dark once more.
  Far down the coast, a light
Flashes and fades again.
  Deep in my heart awakes
The old recurring pain,
  Surges and ebbs once more.

Into the unknown night,
  A boat puts out from shore.

AT 123rd STREET, EAST

I saw them waiting all day in the rain,
Patient and tired and purposeful,
Beating against the door in vain.
Grizzled old men with twisted, shrunken limbs,
Small boys on crutches; score on score
Of huddled women, each one with a child.

Then, from the vantage of a doorway opposite,
Beyond the second-story window glass
I saw a burly, bearded figure pass
And stoop above a bed. I saw his hands
Poised . . . More I could not see.
But when he rose and moved away again,
A woman held a tiny figure up
And dressed the child with trembling, practiced
    hands,
Kissing the tiny shoulder, the warm neck,
And the wide eyes already come to wear
That bright and puzzled look of constant pain.

Traffic thundered down the avenue,
Dull morning waned and duller twilight fell.
And still they came, misshapen, halt and lame.
My mind was groping for a vagrant phrase.
Something to do with children and with them
Who came to touch a certain garment's hem,
Something about "such faith in Israel."

Two college boys strode by, paused for a bit,
Their splendid bodies hunched against the rain.
One said, shame-faced, "Say—like the Bible, isn't it?"

CONVALESCENT

Shy wind in the grasses,
  Soft bloom on the tree,
Gray gulls that go over
  To find the sea.

Like liquid silver
  The pines among,
Poignant to heartbreak
  A sparrow song.

New strength for to-morrow
  And work again.
Banished behind me
  Yesterday's pain.

Shy wind in the grasses,
  The sun's clean kiss;
I might have had heaven
  But I chose this.

CATHEDRAL DOORWAY

Lame, leprous, mutilated, halt, and blind,
The beggars stretch their claws into the light.
"God give you health," they say, "God send you
    luck,"
"God guard your sight!"

SPORT O'KINGS

Charley's Boy and *Tombeyoola,*
Hindustan and *Bill and Coo;*
Superbum and *Copper Demon,*
Bacchus, War God, Cockatoo.

Lord, I read 'em in the subway,—
Printed names upon a page;
Till my heart is like an eagle
Prisoned in a narrow cage.

Colleen, Mickey Moore, Acushla,
Blarney Stone and *Canny Miss;*
Kelly, Kenmare, Little Patsy,
Irish Dawn and *Dream* and *Kiss.*

Ah, the good names from the Gaelic,
How my heart forgets its load
To the sound of flying hoof-beats
Thudding down the Limerick Road!

Boots and Saddle, Knight o' Heather,
Sunbrae, Gondolier, Grandee;
Eagle's Plume and *Water Willow,*
Port Light, Moonrise, Romany.

Sure they take the heart outdoors, Lad,
And they lift it as with wings.
Their names are horns hallooing
To the ancient sport of kings.

Luck and *Charity, Five Aces,*
Vengeance, Smile Again, You Bet;
Winall, Better Times, Freebooter,
Play-boy, Monsoon, Martinet.

Timid days are on the country,
But while gambling blood runs red,
We shall drink one toast together,
"Gentlemen, the thoroughbred!"

149

MOVIE MAGIC

It is November and the skies are cold,
An icy wind whirls down the dingy street;
A beggar hobbles by on crippled feet.
The world and I are very, very old.

Faintly I hear the call of violins,
A motley gathering seeks the picture show;
Into that house of shadow-shapes I go.
The unreal ceases and the real begins.

A small boy whoops aloud in ecstasy;
A woman draws a single sobbing breath
To see adventure grappling there with Death,
Romance come face to face with Mystery.

And when at last the wedding bells are rung,
(Short intermission; You may keep your seat.)
Homeward I swing down starlit, singing streets,
Ho, heart of mine! The world and I are young.

A CHRISTMAS CARD

Two little Christmas trees green at the portal,
And one little card but it says so much:
It tells you that love goes the long way my heart
    knows,
Home "to the low door that laughs to my touch."

NEW LAMPS

(Class poem, University of Maine, 1915)

Today we stand at the crossroads, with
    loath yet eager feet,
Misty before us the future lies, radiant
    and sweet,
Aglow with promises vague and dear and
    rich in its possible lore;
But we turn our eyes from its glory to
    gaze at the past once more.
June rules the good green earth today;
    she strews with lavish hands
Bird song and leaf and drift o'bloom,
    gifts for a king's command—
But our hearts remember a fairer day,
    silvered with autumn rain,
When we sighted first thy dear dim
    walls, O Alma Mater, Maine!
The bend of the blue Stillwater; broken
    logs slipping by,
Comradely shouts of greeting, exultant,
    wild and high,
The lonely, homesick throb in the
    throat; the strangeness of it all,
Then the Stein Song surging like a sea
    against the chapel wall.

Our road has been royal after all, its
  borders green and sweet,
Life has showered her graces; her
  largess has been complete.
But now she lifts a haughty hand and
  stays our feet a space,
And we glimpse in this, our triumph
  hour, the sternness of her face.
As she speaks with the voice of the
  weary world: "My gifts have
  been fair and free,
Youth and unrest and the comrade-
  heart, now what will you give to me?"
Youth and unrest and the comrade-
  heart create our answer bold,
Dauntless we fling life's challenge
  back: "We give new lamps for old,
New Lamps for the world's old darkness, flame of divinest fire,
New for old and for tinsel, gold and the
  dream for the dead desire!"
Father, we lift our lamps to Thee, O
  kindle Thou the flame!
Shelter it Lord from storms of doubt,
  guard it from breath of shame,
Temper the winds of wrath, O Lord,
  and lift the shadow of fear,
Feed our lamps with the oil of faith,
  keep them serene and clear.

Words we have never heeded, Lord,
    assail our memories now,
Our careless hands have found their work;
    that work establish Thou!
Grant Thou, Lord, in a darkened world,
    we keep our lamps alight,
Grant that the flame at least be clear
    if it may not yet be bright,
Grant that we pay our debt to life re-
    turning her largess free,
Kindle Thou, Father, the sacred flame,
    We lift our lamps to thee.
Maine, give strength to my children,
    reverence and awe,
Let them dispel the dark of crime with
    the cleansing torch of law.
Men shall go forth from here today,
    bearing in careful hands,
Lamps to glow with healing flame, soft
    over ravaged lands,
Where our brothers sing as they fight,
    today; to us it is but a game,
War we call it; the fearful odds are
    death and despair and shame.
So pray that the flame be constant,
    unflickering, staunch and sure,
Pray that its priests be worth their
    trust, steadfast and wholly pure,

Deaf to the claims of party greed, blind
    to the lust of power,
Pray that thy children's children,
    Maine, may see white Peace in flower.
Because thy sons have kept the faith,
    tending in reverent awe,
Holding high in a world corrupt, the
    mighty lamp of law!
Give to thy children visions, Maine—
    visions to the eyes
Of thy farmer-sons who would make
    the earth another Paradise.
The light that glows in the dim of
    dawn, golden-green and red,
The light that runs over rippling wheat
    where impalpable feet have sped,
The breath of spring-time orchards,
    adrift with fragrant snow.
The scent of fresh-turned furrows, row
    after warm brown row,
The sight of leaves uncurling, the hush
    of blessed rain,
Glowing and hard-won harvests, orderly
    sheaves of grain,
Because of thy sons, O Mother, shall
    the world behold anew,

Because they have sowed their seeds in
    faith have kept their furrows
    true,
Because in triumph sturdy, agriculture's
    strong lamp glows,
The wilderness smiles and the desert
    shall blossom like the roses!
Maine, thrill the hearts of thy children
    with eternal boyish zeal,
That thine engineers may hold as toys
    their marble, stone and steel.
Men shall go forth from here today,
    with compass, rule and rod,
Igniting flames to shine serene on pathways
    still untrod.
Frowning mountain battlements shall
    know its dauntless glow,
Where a silver curve of railroad climbs
    to eternal snow,
Fevered tropic jungles shall wither in
    its blast,
Men who go down to the sea in ships,
    shall know their danger past,
Because of a golden finger that knows
    not night or fear,
Beckoning to adventure, the lamp of
    the engineer
Shall find undreamed-of thoroughfares
    whose dust no man has trod—
Far-calling hidden highways to lead
    the world to God!

Maine, in the souls of thy children,
    perpetuate thy truth,
Let Science and Art remain for us in
    eternal, splendid youth,
To the hands of each entrusted, some
    precious, pure, lamp glows.
We have marked the path of the bird
    in air, have pierced the heart of
    the rose;
Have drawn from the veins of our
    mother-earth sure anodyne for
    pain,
Our alchemy is white art now that
    seeks another's gain;
Whatsoever things are lovely and of
    good report and pure
Those things thou hast taught us only,
    thy worship is secure.
We thirst for beauty; not in vain thou
    hast sought our thirst to slake,
Science and Art we will follow still for
    their own immortal sake!
Father, we lift our lamps to Thee. Oh,
    kindle Thou the flame!
Shelter it, Lord, from storms of doubt,
    guard it from breath of shame,
Temper the winds of wrath, O Lord,
    and lift the shadow of fear,
Feed our lamps with the oil of faith,
    keep them serene and clear.

Words we have never heeded, Lord,
    assail our memories now,
Our careless hands have found their
    work: that work, establish Thou!
Grant Thou, Lord, in a darkened world
    we keep our lamps alight,
Grant that the flame at least be clear,
    if it may not yet be bright,
Grant that we pay our debt to Life,
    returning her largess free,
Kindle Thou, Father, the sacred flame—
    we lift our lamps to Thee!

            —ELIZABETH HANLY.

*(Copied verbatim from Bangor Daily News of
June 8, 1915—p. 15)*